Kristian!!
My sister!
Rock On!

It's YOUR Business

Good Stuff for Your
Personal, Professional, and Funny Business

by Speaker Hall of Fame Inductee
Christine Holton Cashen, MAEd, CSP

Copyright © 2017 Christine Holton Cashen. All rights reserved.

No part of this book may be used or reproduced in any manner without express written permission, excepting brief quotations embodied in articles and reviews.

For bulk purchases, call 214.395.3506

Published by DC Murphy Publishing, Dallas, Texas

Edited by Debbie Johnson, Spike Communications, www.SpikeCommunications.com
Book Design by Formation Studio, www.FormationStudio.com

First Edition, Printed in the USA

ISBN-978-0-9829751-2-1

Dedicated to YOU...

This book is for all of you optimists out there,
who choose happiness amidst a sea of critics.
When most people are focused on problems, you are focused on solutions.
This book is dedicated to those of you who keep smiling and moving forward,
with grace in your step and a smile on your face!

It's YOUR Business

TABLE OF CONTENTS

1 Positivity Rocks
Pg 2

2 Oh My, Simplify!
Pg 46

3 Surviving Those Fast Balls
Pg 58

4 Living in the Moment
Pg 78

5 Appreciat-cha!
Pg 106

It's YOUR Business

Positivity Rocks

1

In Good Company [with Water Woman]

My son had his heart set on a strawberry birthday cake with a race track decoration — nothing too extreme. So off we went to the local grocery store bakery.

Bakery Babe: "I'm sorry, we only have chocolate and vanilla cakes."

Tired Mom: "Really?!?"

Clueless Bakery Babe: "No one around here makes a strawberry cake."

Irritated Mom: "How about *The Flour Shop* — that specialty cupcake place down the street?"

Helpful Baker: "Oh yes, they would. They are the best. You should get your cake from them."

Resigned Mom: "Thanks, we will."

Birthday Boy: "Well, that was unusual. Why is she giving her business to someone else?"

Motivational Speaker Mom: "She doesn't think of it as her business."

Birthday Boy: "But this is where she works. That doesn't make sense. Let's check out and try somewhere else."

Checkout Dude: "Is that La Croix water any good?"

Still Tired Mom: "Yes, I love it. It is a great alternative to pop, and I love the lime."

Random Shopper at Next Checkout: "Did you know Perrier has lime bubble water in cans?"

Confused Mom: "What? Who? What?"

Let me cut to the chase. This woman is wearing a baseball cap and sweats, and is clearly not on the clock. She dumps her cart and comes over to tell me she works for Perrier and wants me to try *her water*. She asks me to wait and sprints away, only to come back with 2 cases of Perrier and 1 case of San Pellegrino (also owned by Perrier). She swipes her corporate card and puts the water in my cart. She told me to ask for it at restaurants and left to go pay for her items.

I was dumbfounded. I turned to my son, *"Now, that is owning your business... and it is her day off!"*

LOTS TO PONDER

What kind of employee are you? Clueless Bakery Babe or Water Woman (my hero!)?

Which one would you want working for you?

Who do you want to do business with?

What would customer service be like if everyone approached their job as if it were their own business?

HOT TIP

Empower your people.
Get Empowered.
And, keep good company.

Do Not Feed the Trolls

The word Troll has had many meanings over the years. Where I grew up in Michigan, those in the Upper Peninsula called those who lived "under" the Mackinac Bridge (Lower Peninsula), Trolls. To Troll downtown, meant to "check it out." Trolling is also a method of fishing. Do you remember the Troll dolls? I have had hair days like that. Fast forward... now there is a new meaning... a Troll is someone who makes nasty comments on social media.

JASON GOES TO TARGET

My wonderful friend Jason wrote a blog about seeing his wife at Target, not realizing it was her, and falling for her all over again. The opener on his Facebook post was priceless: he explains that he saw this gorgeous woman while he was shopping and felt like he was cheating on his wife… only to realize it was her! It was such a beautiful and honest open love letter to his wife that was shared all over the place, going viral with more than 145k shares. Ironically, his wife doesn't often go on Facebook, and he suspected she'd never even see the post unless he told her about it.

CUE THE HATERS

But something happened. This beautiful story abruptly goes sideways! Suddenly total strangers begin posting mean-spirited comments. What's not to love here? Why would anyone do this?!? Somehow I got caught up reading these awful comments amongst the supportive and kind remarks. Have you ever read a story, then gone down the wormhole, reading all the comments? I felt so downtrodden — like I'd just discovered that the world is a harsh and cruel place, populated by venomous people with poison in their hearts.

Positivity Rocks | *It's YOUR Business* | 7

SIMON SAYS
Another example is my friend's juggling duo. They actually made it to the semi-finals... of *America's Got Talent*. Talented performers and amazing human beings they are. Once again, the Trolls rear their ugly (probably non-talented) heads.

Apparently, the feeling of being anonymous gives these Trolls an odd sense of power. These are the same people who are probably in terrible relationships or are alone in their parents' basements feeling miserable. I had to sit on my hands not to defend my friends against these haters, because I know deep down that I will not change the minds of any of these people. Politics anyone?

KINDNESS IS THE NEW BLACK
The truth is that hurt people want to hurt people. Loved people want to love on people. Whenever you see these nasty comments from Trolls, do not engage. I repeat, do not engage. Just make sure you don't add fuel to the fire. Think before you click. Ask yourself, "Is what I am about to say kind, helpful, or supportive?" Do not feed the Trolls. Starve them.

Let's face it. The world needs ***fewer critics*** and ***more cheerleaders.*** **Go Team Kindness!**

Reservations About Humor?

When people think about humor, it usually relates to telling jokes, or situations where you double over in laughter. To me it's more than that — it's about having (and making) fun in the ordinary and often dull routines in everyday life.

CHOCOLATE RUN

For example, after dropping the kids off at school, I dread coming home to the disaster in my kitchen. Often times while cleaning up breakfast dishes and lunch prep chaos, our chocolate lab will plop down nearby with a heavy sigh.

In my effort to put off re-combobulating the kitchen for as long as possible, I call his name — Murphy — and then I hide behind the counter. When he scrambles to his feet, a chase around the center island ensues. Yes, I play Hide & Seek with my dog. Don't judge me. It's great fun and gets the blood flowing — for both of us.

A ROSE BY ANY OTHER NAME

Another fave in our family is the "Restaurant Name-Game." Last week, I took my son on a lunch date to one of our favorite places, Which Wich. You build your own sandwich, turn in your order, and write your name on the bottom of the bag. For kicks, we always put random names, like "Batman," "Jim Shortz," or "Tired Puppy" (that one would be mine). It is always a kick when the young employee yells out in a bland voice, "I have a turkey for... Tired Puppy."

This can also backfire. My brother and his wife were going out for an anniversary dinner and made reservations at their favorite restaurant. Also a goofball, he made the reservation using the name "Hungry," and mentioned this was a special evening. After the meal, the server brought them a complimentary dessert with (in chocolate writing), "Happy Anniversary Mr. and Mrs. Hungry!"

How can you add fun to your daily routine? One thing is for certain — humor makes memories. Figure out ways to make the mundane into something memorable.

MY NAME Jim Shortz
MY WICH WICKED

MY NAME Batman

○ *Philly* **CHEESESTEAK**
Thinly sliced steak, caramelized onions, sautéed bell peppers, and melted provolone on a toasted baguette

○ **ITALIAN CLUB**
Thinly sliced turkey breast, spicy capicola, smoked thick-cut bacon, provolone, fresh pesto, lettuce, and tomato on a toasted baguette

○ **MEATBALL GRINDER**
Italian meatballs, Genoa salami, pepperoni, spicy capicola, marinara, mushrooms, and mozzarella on a toasted baguette

MY NAME Tired Puppy
MY WICH
○ Chicken Salad
○ Egg Salad
○ Club

HOT TIP

Figure out ways to make the mundane into something memorable. Get out there and use humor to make the ordinary extraordinary!

Are You Wearing Gotcha Goggles?

We're on the expressway. We've been following a truck for some time and the HOW'S MY DRIVING? sign keeps staring back at me. I remark to my son, "Thank goodness mommy doesn't have a sign on her car asking people to call about her driving!" He seemed happy about that too, much to my chagrin.

FREEWAY FEEDBACK

So, what happens when you call that phone number? Have you ever wondered? Have you ever called? Are you getting ahead of me here? Oh yes, I had to do it.

"Thank you for calling our dedicated safety driving hotline. Please leave the number of the truck, your location, and the incident." Incident?

"Umm... Hi, my name is Christine and I am on Interstate 35 near Hebron Parkway and truck number 364 is driving great! He is maintaining the speed limit, making safe lane changes, and using his turn signal. How's his driving you ask? Excellent!" I even left my name and number so they wouldn't think it was a prank.

GET YOUR SHIFT STRAIGHT

We live in such a "Gotcha" world, constantly looking for things to go wrong. When you have your "Gotcha Goggles" on, you will see plenty of infractions. Try putting on "Grateful Glasses" for a change.

A great tip from my book, *"The Good Stuff,"* is to take the "Ten Coin Challenge." When you get dressed, put 10 coins in your left pocket and begin your day looking for something good to comment on. I know! This may be difficult, but do it anyway.

Tell your partner how much you appreciated finding the newspaper on the kitchen table. Thank your kids for getting themselves up on time. Now here's the change part… each time you appreciate someone, move a coin from your left pocket to your right. Please be subtle so no one knows what you are doing.

CHANGE FOR CHANGE

By the end of the day, you should have all the coins in your right pocket. Full coin transfer may not happen every day, but if you get in the habit of looking through your Grateful Glasses, you'll definitely notice your attitude and attitudes of those around you shifting — in a positive way. When you look for the good, you will find it more often.

Right now, be grateful that you don't have a sign on your car with a phone number asking about *your* driving. Then again, maybe we'd all drive better if we did!

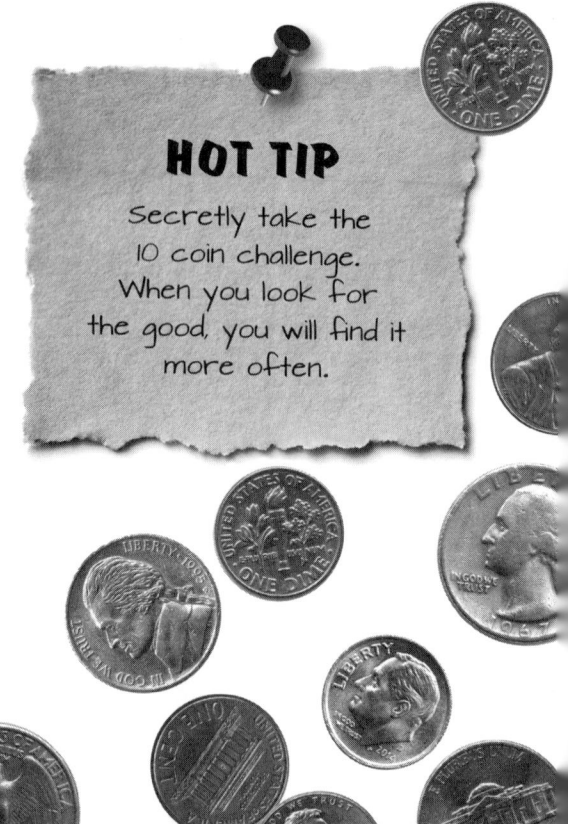

> **HOT TIP**
> Secretly take the 10 coin challenge. When you look for the good, you will find it more often.

Gaga Lesson

A few years ago, there was a ruckus with Lady Gaga at a Mets game. Apparently, she had an issue with her seat location as well as the annoying paparazzi. Irritated, she stripped down to her metal studded leather bikini and gave booing Mets fans a double thumbs up. Wait a minute... those weren't her thumbs. Anyway, as I began to judge her, I started thinking about what it would be like to have everything in your life recorded.

YOUR PANTS ARE CALLING

Have you ever pocket dialed someone or been the recipient of that kind of call? You know, when after saying hello 10 times, you realize the person dialed you accidentally? I often hear my mom yelling my name from my pocket or handbag. It always freaks me out.

Have you also noticed that for some twisted reason, upon figuring out that you are the recipient of a "butt dial," you continue listening like a creepy voyeur? Yeah… I've done it.

Maybe you caught someone yelling at the dog, talking smack, or singing off key to the car radio? How would you alter behavior knowing your partner, kids, friends, or boss was listening?

VIDEO KILLED THE RADIO STAR

At a birthday party, we hosted 18 elementary school kids at a local pool. A handful of parents stayed for the romp, but many escaped. It was wild with kids dripping wet, running amok, hurling cannon balls on unsuspecting swimmers, and the random, "Umm… Mrs. Cashen, I can't find my underwear."

The whole scene had me pretty wound up. Towards the end of the party, we gave every kid a "noodle" as a gift and all hell broke loose. Picture 18 sugared-up kids running around using pool noodles as swords, horses and bats. Yes, a small freak-out did occur. Not the kids… me! There is nothing quite like seeing a motivational speaker melt down. *Who is that hot mess? Oh, she is the one who speaks across the country about having less stress and more fun in your life.* Great.

No, I didn't strip down to a studded leather bikini, curse anyone, or flip the bird. But if I did, at least it wouldn't have made the news. That incident sure made me think. How would you act if you knew you were being filmed? Thank goodness I was the only one at the party filming, and I put the phone down before I flipped out.

SMILE — YOU'RE ON YOUTUBE

I'm not condoning what the pop diva did at the Mets game. What I'm saying is that we should lay off judging too harshly — lest we spend a day in Gaga's metal studded bikini. We all have our meltdown moments. Obviously, some are more outrageous than others. Often times we don't know the real story behind someone's behavior, and we have no idea what it would be like to be in a constant spotlight. However, in this era of all things video, a good rule to follow is: always act like those you care about, admire, and respect are watching, because they just might be! If you're going to be a viral sensation, make it a proud moment.

I Can See Clearly Now — The Fear is Gone!

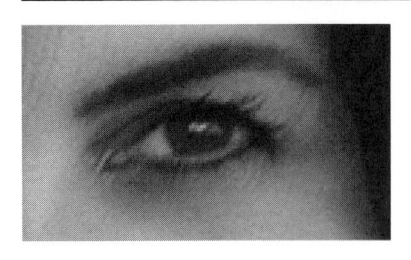

After many years of sticking plastic lenses in my eyes, I developed an allergy to my contacts. Can you say, "Owieeeee??!?" Lasik always sounded like the way to go, but fear always got the best of me. No longer able to wear contacts, I researched doctors, did the whole pre-screen thing, and had the surgery DONE (really!) within a week (I knew that waiting and thinking about it would mess with my head.)

So here I am a few weeks later, seeing better than ever and wondering why I didn't do this sooner. When I squint my right eye, I can hear the famous Steve Austin, *"do-do-do-do-do"* (bionic eye sound effect). If you don't know what that is, ask your parents.

The whole experience got me thinking about how fear holds us back. Some guru once said that the acronym for fear is *False Evidence Appearing Real*. I don't know about that... having a laser beam drill into my eyes is real... scary... real scary. But, I had to deal and move forward — because I was forced to make the change.

How often do we have blurred vision without knowing it? We begin to believe that the blur is normal and live with it. It usually isn't until we get out of the situation that we see things more clearly. Why didn't I leave that job earlier? Why didn't I get out of that relationship sooner? Why didn't I get Lasik a long time ago? Are you seeing things clearly right now? What is holding you back? Fear? Lack of money? Confidence? Why does change have to be forced upon us to realize it is what we wanted all along?

POSITIVE FUTURE FOCUS

Ask yourself, "What is possible?" and play only to the positive. Too often, we focus only on the negative outcomes. What if I ask for a raise, and I get it? What if I ask my partner to be home from work every day at 6:30, so we can eat together as a family, and it actually happens?!

NO RISK... NO REWARD

If you are risk adverse, try chanting, "Ohhhhh what the heckkkk, gooooo for it anywayyyyy." You will never know the outcome until you try. If it doesn't work, you are no worse off than before, and at least you can move in another direction.

FORGET NEW YEAR'S RESOLUTIONS

Making goals once a year? Forgettaboutit! It is easy to get down on yourself the very first week. Most people give up by March. "Oh well, there's always next year." What? Even if you blew it, you can still do it! Reset your thinking at the beginning of *every* month. Yell, "Happy New Month," and refocus your efforts. Are you really wanting to rock your resolutions? Yell, "Happy New Week," and start off Mondays with a bang rather than a sputter. Truly, every day is a new start. Right now I can hear Scarlett O'Hara saying, "After all... tomorrow is another day!" and she is right.

THINK IT AND INK IT

Write down what you want to accomplish and keep it in front of your eyes. This will help you set your internal GPS. It is certainly easier to get to your destination when you have a map. Especially, those of you who never ask for directions — you know who you are. Recalculating....

> **HOT TIP**
> Write down what you want to accomplish and keep it in a visible location.

PARTNER ANYONE?

Find an accountability partner who can keep you motivated and on task. A friend and I are on a health kick, and it is fun to check-in at night to see how we did. She offers great suggestions and also makes me feel better by sharing that she snuck some chocolate too.

So open your eyes right now and move toward what you want, while steering clear of what you don't. Make a plan and don't give up. We are all afraid... feel the fear and do it anyway. Have a clear vision, focus and get your life in gear... starting today. You will see clearly when the fear is gone. Do I hear that bionic eye sound effect?

Mood Poisoning Epidemic

Watch out, be careful, and on high alert — it can happen anywhere and anytime... your mood can be poisoned. You can be zipping along enjoying your day and run across a jerky person and WHAM! Instantly you are in a foul mood. Sometimes this lasts for about an hour. Other times it can last days, months, or even YEARS. You know you have mood poisoning when "things just aren't that funny" anymore, criticizing others becomes a sport, and you have an uncanny urge to slap happy people.

Positivity Rocks | It's YOUR Business | 21

Try These 8 Great Mood Poisoning Remedies:

1. Go on a news fast. Get your update once a day to keep current. If something major is going on, someone will tell you.

2. Make up a story about a toxic person's past. Hurt people want to hurt people. Don't let the effects of their mood poisoning infect you.

3. Stave off negative people with a smile. It is amazing how you can change an encounter with something so simple. Greeting people with a smile almost always changes an interaction for the better. As a bonus, you also change your attitude when you change your face.

4 When someone is complaining, be a good listener, but try to move the conversation to something more positive. Mood poisoning always gets worse when you try to beat someone's rotten story with one of your own. Pity party table for two? Sorry, no reservations!

5 If you are bummed about your own circumstances, plan to make some changes in your life. Seek advice from others and never give up. Every day do one or two things to move toward your goal.

6 Connect with someone you care about. Picking up the phone and calling a friend or loved one you haven't spoken to in a while can be a great blues buster.

7 Help someone else. Volunteer. Do a random act of kindness. Not only is it a good thing to do, it is tonic for the soul.

8 Don't walk away from negative people — RUN! Hide that Facebook friend who always has a status of doom. Surround yourself with people who bring energy rather than drain it from you.

SELF INFLICTED?

Sometimes you don't get mood poisoning from other people, you do it to yourself! It is easy to get into a funk over your weight, money, relationships, etc. These days I find myself getting news overload about the "INSERT CURRENT NEWS SPECTACLE HERE." I watch the TV coverage, then hit the internet for more depth and up-to-date coverage. Then to add insult to injury, I dive into all the comments regarding said event. What am I thinking? At that point my stomach hurts and I'm wanting to insert a sharp stick in my eye. Ah-ha! News Poisoning!

STILL SLAP HAPPY?

Protect yourself and others from the effects of Mood Poisoning. This epidemic is preventable, and it is your obligation to do your part. If you still have the urge to slap happy people, please go back and try the eight great ideas again. On the other hand, there are options. You may want to seek help from a professional. Try doing five jumping jacks and see if that helps. Or you can pull the covers over your head, grab magazines and chocolate, and plan for tomorrow to be better than today!

Seven Habits of Highly Annoying People (H.A.P.)

I'm not quite sure if it's the full moon or too much time on the road (perhaps a little of both) that has made me especially sensitive to certain peoples' habits. I joke about the "rule breakers" of society in my presentations, but it seems like they were out in force as if to test me. Have you seen any H.A.P. recently? Turn the page to see if you recognize any of these annoyances (I'm sure it's not you!).

1. Public Grooming

While walking through the airport, I heard a pinging noise. My ears perked up as I recognized the offensive sound of nail clippers. As if out of a scene in a horror movie, I turn to see a woman with her knee hiked up under her chin, CLIPPING HER TOE NAILS in the middle of Concourse C, Gate 27 seating area. *shutter*

Whether brushing their hair, flossing their teeth, or plucking their chin hairs, these self-groomers don't miss an opportunity to do things in public that most of us only do in the privacy of our own bathrooms!

2. The "One-Upper"

No matter what you say, they have a similar story or an even better story to share with you. "Oh you think that is embarrassing? Well, let me tell you...." When they are done, I always want to whip out my story about the time I wore my lavalier microphone to the bathroom during a seminar. Even though that embarrassing story beats most, I try to let the one-upper bask in the glory and just empathize with them about their event.

Can't anyone just enjoy a story without having to have the last word? I know... sometimes it's all about bonding... you share your story and then I share mine. But if you do this all the time, most likely you're part of the H.A.P. scene.

3. Taking Calls / Checking E-mail When Someone is Talking to You

I'm sure these people are great at multi-tasking, but it sure makes you feel like a non-priority when this happens. Everyone is wearing a sign that says, "Make me look good and make me feel important." When people whip out their phones, they are wearing a sign that says, *"I'm working on something more important than you."*

4. Letting Your Kids Run Wild

Hey, I have kids and understand how difficult it can be sometimes, but dang, people, control your children in public! At the Post Office recently, a man let his little one use the Automated Postal Machine as a toy. He was punching and pushing buttons over and over until the screen said *Out of Order*. I kept looking at the kid, then glaring at the Dad. I was thinking of all the things I could say that would be a teaching moment for the kid and a light bulb moment for the Dad — without offending him, of course. Nothing good was going to come out of my mouth, so I stood there like a raging mute while the Dad continued to calmly look around without a care in the world. If you can't control them now, look out for their teenage years and pity the public who has to deal with the fallout.

5. Clueless Driving

Make your car a no cell phone zone and pay attention! Most of us are on auto pilot as it is, so we don't need something else to take our minds off the driving task at hand. There are far too many driving rules and regs to even list, but here are a few of my personal faves: use your turn signal; if you are not going faster than me in the left lane, move over; and if someone lets you merge, please give that kind person the "thank you" wave.

Recently, I pulled up to a strip mall and parked. I opened the door, and was gathering myself, and trying to gather my kids. Out of the back, I notice a woman sitting in her car waiting to park next to us. Down the line, there were eight other OPEN parking spots! Did she really have to use the one next to the hot-mess mom trying to get it together? We all could use the extra steps on our fitness trackers. Hmmm… maybe you don't always need the closest parking spot.

6. Being Unaware of Your Surroundings

I would say, you know who you are — but obviously you don't. Loud cell phone talkers. Non-deciders who stand at the bottom of the escalator, not sure which way to go. Those who leave their shopping carts in the middle of the grocery store aisle, and those in the express line with far too many items. There are other people in the world. Notice them, and act with consideration.

7. Whining

I'm at the airport. While waiting to get on the standby list, I was hanging out at the counter, people watching. This was a very interesting scene because the gate agent was one tough cookie. She was making sure everyone's bag fit easily into the "bag sizer," which is a form (approximately 22" x 14" x 9") that your bag must fit into easily if you plan to carry it on your flight rather than check it. As a frequent traveler, let me tell you that 90% of carry on bags do not fit in the "sizer," but are able to fit in the overhead compartment (with some extra shoving-a-hem).

Well, all these well-appointed business travelers were in shock over having to check their oversized bags. Every one of them either whined about "traveling every week and never checking once" or whipped out a gold status card to prove the point. They were frustrated (as I would be) and felt that arguing with the gate agent would change her mind. Wrong. It didn't work for the first 20 people to board, why would it work for you? Yeah, it wasn't really fair, but life isn't always so fair. Put on your big boy boxers or big girl bloomers and get on with it. It is what it is and you don't always get your way. It bears repeating: Join the mission to Stop Global Whining. There is a lot of tragedy in the world — waiting for your suitcase at baggage claim doesn't qualify.

THEY KNOW NOT WHAT THEY DO

Here's the real deal. Most Highly Annoying People and their habits are not out to annoy you. They are just annoying. Most people know not what they do. Instead of our criticism, disgust, and judgment, they truly need our love, prayers, and support. We all need more of that these days. So please give the H.A.P. a break because maybe one day the Highly Annoying Person will be YOU.

> **HOT TIP**
> Lighten up! We're all just hot messes trying to do the best we can.

Status Brand: Boost Your Post Profile

SAME SUBJECT DIFFERENT DAY

What does your Facebook status say about you? If you were to make a list of your status posts from the last six months, a profile would appear. Is there a trend? Are all of your posts concerning the same topic?

Now, don't get all sensitive and defensive — hear me out. Trying not to be judgmental here, but are all your posts regarding your health? Your relationship? Your kids? Your work? Come on, mix it up a bit! Be clever, pithy, interesting, or maybe wait until you are these things before just randomly typing.

Many of you know what I'm talking about. Those posts that are always in the same category that make us (me) hover over the "hide" button. Have you ever gotten so fed up that you've taken the extreme UNFRIEND route? Don't let this happen to you! The point of Facebook is to keep connected in this increasingly disconnected world. Don't be a one-hit poster.

Positivity Rocks / *It's YOUR Business*

Check Out These Prevalent Post Categories:

The Cryptic	*"Oh no, not again." "Can't take much more." "Seriously?!"* Cryptics are just begging for people to inquire into their mysterious lives.
Kid-Driven	*"Here is another cute quote from my little genius." "Wow, 10 soccer games this weekend and I'm beat!"* I didn't know you played soccer... oh wait, it isn't you... it's your kid.
Taskers	*"I am now writing a blog." "I just went to the bathroom." "Are you holding your breath wondering what I'm going to do next?!"*
Quoters	*"Thanks for quoting me."* – Ben Franklin
MLMers	*"Buy my product." "Join the pyramid under me."* And the ever popular, *"Let me invite you to a party/event."* Sorry... can't come to your kitchen gadget shin-dig. I live on another continent. H-E-L-L-O?!
Spoilers	*"I can't believe Cheryl was booted!" "My favorite chef Kenny was just sent home!" "If you are DVRing a reality show, I will save you the time and post about it."* This is especially a bummer for the West Coasters.
Body Reporters	*"My throat still hurts." "I can't stop sneezing." "I wish you could smell this."*
Self Promoters	*"After reading this post, check out my book on www.christinecashen.com/shop"* (couldn't resist).

Ghost Poster	I can't think of my own clever thing, so I'm going to use a site to get something fun to post. Don't repost. Be your authentic self.
Gamers	*"I need some milk for my baby goat." "I need a rifle." "I need a rifle to kill a goat."*
Foodies	You know who these people are. They show pictures of artistically-plated food and half-finished cocktails. I always want to take a picture of my lame dinner and post it in retaliation.
Buzzkills	*"I have the worst luck ever." "Didn't sleep at all last night." "Nothing ever goes right for me."* Come join my pity party.
Cause Reposters	*"This is National Hangnail support week. If you or someone you know has a hangnail, be supportive."* Another one is, *"This week is hug your dog week."* Who determines what week is for what cause? Maybe your time would be better spent volunteering for your favorite cause rather than reposting.
Sporties	*"Dang Lions!" "If you are DVRing the game, let me spoil it for you."* *See Spoilers*
Political Ranters	*"Join the tea party!" "Join the coffee party." "Please send a check."*
Weekend Warriors	*"Is it Friday yet?" "Two more days till the weekend." "I wish my life didn't revolve around only TWO days of the week!"*

Positivity Rocks | It's YOUR Business | 33

WHO ARE YOU?

See yourself in this random sampling? Again, if you are in multiple categories, good for you! If you are posting in just one area, I challenge you to break out and try something new. Most people you are "friends" with are just getting this random glimpse of you and your life. What do you really want to share? Do you want to make them smile? Give them something good to think about? Share some cool facts about you and what is happening?

The advent of social media truly allows you to create your own brand, whether you know it or not. Remember, many of us have more than "friends" on our list. There are co-workers, employers, and clients all peeking into your lives.

Some people contend that they are not in business, so it doesn't matter. Wrong! You are in business — the business of your life. Yes, it does matter because you are the CEO of you!

Be careful and boost your brand, baby. And if you get the chance, boost the brands of others. Break out of the post doldrums. Just like breakfast, most of us want variety. Have fun and happy posting!

Talk Show No-Go

It's some people's guilty pleasure, and some people's trashy treasure. There is a hostile takeover of the airwaves by sleazy television shows (affectionately called "Junk TV" in our house) — and I almost got sucked into the moral vacuum. Most reality and talk shows are like car accidents. You don't want to look, but you can't help yourself! Turn it off. No! Maybe I'll just watch a bit longer. OFF! No! Has this ever happened to you? You pass by a show and end up indulging in the insanity — but just for a few minutes. And then a few MORE minutes? This is followed by disbelief that you wasted the last (insert ridiculous number) minutes of your life that you will never get back. Where is a memory erase device when you need it? But, I digress.

WHERE DO THEY GET THESE PEOPLE?

What would you be willing to do to be "famous?" Recently, I had an opportunity to find out. A reporter put out a query looking for someone who has a meddling mom to be a guest on a new talk show. Quick background: I have an amazing mom. She is my best friend. She is Italian.

She is a meddler. I could give you many meddling examples, but this one tells all — she is on Twitter and I am the ONLY one she follows. Nuff said.

HAVE BANTER WILL TRAVEL

After discussing the show with my mom, we both got giddy at the prospect of an all-expense paid adventure in NYC, so I answered the reporter's query. The Producer contacted me and assured me that this was not a "chair-throwing" type of show; rather, it features human interest stories. She then interviewed us both, had us send pictures and invited us to be on this new show. She explained that it will air in Dallas and Houston this September in hopes of getting full syndication. They wanted me and my "hilarious mom" to have some fun bantering back and forth alongside three other meddling mom duos. For those who know my mom and me, "fun banter" is standard chat. So... NYC, Mom and me, our moment of fame... sounds like fun, right?

REALITY STRIKES

An assistant called to get details for our flight arrangements and had a few additional questions such as, "Do you have tattoos? Piercings? A weave? Gold teeth? A grill?" She wasn't asking about a BBQ, but rather teeth jewelry. WTH?!? At that moment, I get a call from my dad who found clips of the show on a web site (even though it has yet to hit the airwaves). Highlights included someone ranting about a cheating spouse and another clip had the esteemed host getting bleeped out as he was yelling at one of his own guests. What have I gotten us into?

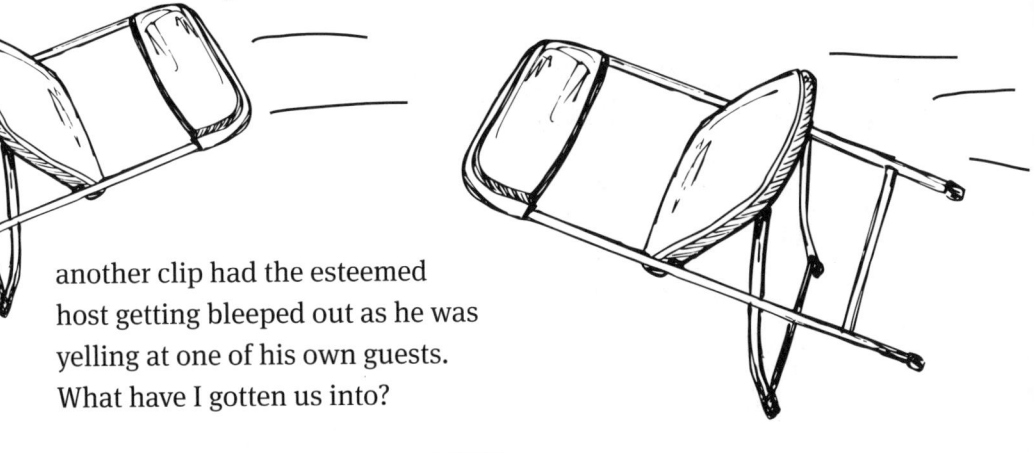

CREATING MY OWN REALITY

The show looked borderline chair tossing to me, and we decided to call the Producer and bow out. There was truly nothing to gain (other than a trip to NYC) and a lot to lose. My reputation, based on laughter and positive living, means more to me than a moment of "fame" if that is what you call it.

It's not just about what you preach, or even what you practice. It's also about the company you keep, what you support, and where you invest your time (and message). Being in the wrong place at the wrong time — even if you do right — ends up all wrong.

So, we're planning a mother/daughter trip to NYC on our own terms. This Housewife of Denton County is out. We're off to discover some GOOD STUFF of our own, even if we have to do our own hair and make-up.

When the Guard Keeps You Up

I may be a perky motivational speaker on stage, but at home in the morning, I am a hard-core drill sergeant. After my sing song "get-out-of-bed-sleepy-head" routine, it is GO TIME.

Typically, I bark orders at my kids, push blueberries, search for papers I need to sign, throw together lunches, and try to tame my daughter's wild lion's mane. Anyone have ideas for curly hair care?

It doesn't get much better when we hit the road. We take the "back way" to school which is pointless because everyone else does too. It's a perilous obstacle course — dodging parked cars, observing annoying driving etiquette rules (you go first, no you go first, no you, wave, smile, repeat), while simultaneously quizzing my son on his recent study guide.

Then I see *HIM*.

Mr. Alton (cue singing angels). He is the crossing guard behind our school.

Looking like a handsome skinny Santa, he smiles broadly and greets all the kids. Yelling, "Hey, I sure do like those socks!" and "I'm so glad to see you this morning!"

On Fridays, he high fives everyone and exhorts, "Get excited for a great day!"

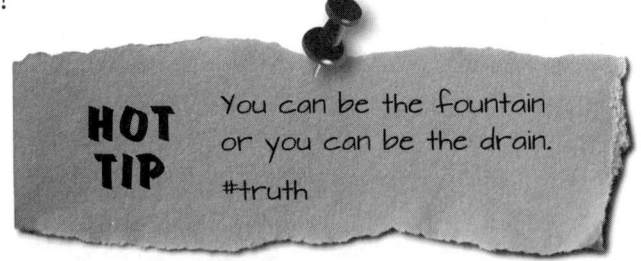

> **HOT TIP**
> You can be the fountain or you can be the drain.
> #truth

Purposely, I slow down to catch his eye so I can wave and catch some of his morning happiness. Just the sight of Mr. Alton brings a smile to my face and to all who encounter him.

And just like that, I AM ready for a great day. How did he do that? Like an Energy Ninja, he slays my bad mood away. Isn't it amazing how energy can be contagious, both good energy and bad energy.

What energy legacy do you leave every day with the people you encounter?

Thanks Mr. Alton, for all the great days!

Stop Cabin Fever Freak Out: Top 10 Indoor Sanity Savers

You are stuck at home. Maybe it's cold and staying cold. Maybe it's 110 degrees and 1000% humidity. Maybe you're under Doctor's orders. What to do? Here are the Top 10 ways to keep your spirits high while you're stuck indoors. Ready, Set…

1. Open that Box. Have you gotten a gift that you have yet to open? This is the perfect time to break the seal on that electronic photo frame or tech gadget you desperately wanted, but can't figure out. Break open the Panini maker or put that juicer to work. Or, if you know you never will, go immediately to #7.

2. Call Your Mother. Or your father, brother, cousin, friend. It's best if they don't live in CA or FL — they will just rub their sunshine in your face. Connect with someone who makes you laugh or someone you haven't talked to in a while. It is the instant pick-me-up.

3. Homestead Olympics! Are the kids stir crazy too? Create an indoor Olympic course and have time trials. Heck, who needs kids? Get wooden spoons and tennis balls to create floor knee hockey. Have you heard about carpet skates? They're out there. Google it!

4. Binge Watch. Are you missing out on those bonding, topical show discussions? Do you have that left-out feeling because you haven't seen *INSERT LATEST NETFLIX HIT HERE?* Couch... Popcorn... Blanket... Marathon... PLAY!

5. Get Neighborly. They probably have cabin fever, too! Check on them if you're doing a grocery run. Maybe a neighborhood card game, potluck, or progressive dinner tonight? You do know your neighbors, right? Get on it!

6. Clean Sweep. What "clutter space" is on your nerves? Pantry? Closet? Has your garage gone wild? You don't have to tackle the whole project, but set the timer for 23 minutes and ROCK, ROLL, and PURGE!

7. Have Goodwill. Grab a bag and fill it! If you have kids, this is the great one. We have toys that haven't been touched in years! Everyone gets a bag and the first one who fills it decides what's for dinner.

8. Kick the Bucket. Get started on one bucket list item. Sign up for that conversational French class. Check out the co-ed adult soccer league. Begin planning your dream vacation.

9. Get Grateful. Write a thank you note. Maybe it goes to a grade school teacher who changed your life, or to that co-worker who always comes in with a great attitude, or to your mechanic who always and miraculously saves your ride from the salvage yard. Yup... pen, paper, stamp.

10. Change up the Grub. I've always wanted to make those Pinterest creations. Grab a cookbook (mine hasn't been touched in years) or jump on a cooking site and break out of that "same-old-same-old" food routine.

So, there you have it. No reason to be bored. When cabin fever strikes, you'll be armed and ready. Pick an idea and execute!

Positivity Rocks | It's YOUR Business | 43

It's YOUR Business

2

Oh My, Simplify!

Deprive to Revive!

There I was, lying in a "sensory awareness" pod, floating in dense salt water. For the first 10 minutes, there is light and the sound of waves. Then darkness, and only the sound of my own breath and heartbeat.

The float was featured at a speaker retreat with the goal of emerging with clarity, peace, and new ideas. The pressure was on. Could I shut my mind off for an hour in hopes of creating something really unique and original? For the first few minutes in the tank I was a bit freaked out, then calm... until the lights went out and then my mind went on overdrive:

What am I going to make for dinner? Stop that. Did I pack the kids' snacks? Relax. I have an itch near my eye. Will I get salt in it if I dare touch it? Just breathe. Why do the Mavericks always lose in overtime? Focus! Dang, what time is it?

Rejoining the group was so disappointing. While my colleagues fiercely scribbled brainstorms, no new ideas surfaced for me and I sat sadly in front of a blank paper. Finally, I wrote the word **"MOMENT."** Then I wrote, "not many moments for mom." Hey, MOM is the first three letters in *MOM*ent! Then, in the middle of moment, I saw ME!

There it was! **We all need to put more ME into our mo*me*nts.** In thinking back, I had a whole bunch of ME time in the float tank, and I couldn't relax. I couldn't focus on my breathing. I couldn't clear my head. The environment was perfect, yet I didn't know how to begin. Scheduling "me" doesn't come naturally for many of us, but hey, come on, let's go for it!

DEPRIVE your mind of all your minutiae. Can you apply brain brakes? Stop dwelling on the past. Stop obsessing over what is next. Stop blaming. Stop checking Instagram (tough!). Step out of the Twitterverse. Quit scheduling. Stop everything except what's going on here and now. For a moment... just be.

STRIVE to be MINDLESS. Yes, you're busy! Calm your brain? Yoga? Meditation? Quiet time? Classical music? Add something different to your "To-Do" list – time for you! Mark your calendar for mind-free time.

REVIVE & THRIVE! Now that you've cleared the decks of your mind, what next? Enjoy your fresh focus! Did you get new ideas? Did clearing chatter help you hear anything new? Put your energy into things that help make your Mojo flow. Then, for cripes sakes, schedule more of those things! Who says you can't plan time each day just for you... don't you deserve it? Listen to the sound of your own breath and heartbeat. You may be surprised at what you hear.

iAddict

Have you ever left your house, happily arrived at your destination, only to have that *where-the-heck-is-my-phone* panic scramble? This includes, but is not limited to: patting down pockets, reaching into bags, completely dumping said bags, and searching under car seat. All the while your eyes are darting around, frozen in time, hoping that a flash will hit, reminding you of your last phone encounter.

Last week I had that panic scramble while out running errands. The unthinkable had occurred: I left my phone at home. Breathing slowly, I told myself that I was only running a few errands. What could go wrong? I reassured myself that I'd soon be reunited with my phone.

While sitting at a red light, I wanted to check my e-mail. Wow, I'm bored. Sheesssh, another red light... where is my blasted phone? Geez, I may look at my phone while driving more than I think. At the UPS store, I waited, wishing I could see what was happening on Twitter. I see a greeting card stand with the usual categories: Birthday, Get Well, Anniversary... wait... what is this? "Almost Funny" cards? Love it! Wish I could take a picture of it... bummer... I forgot my phone. Should I be somewhere? My phone usually alerts me with an alarm for any appointments or conference calls. For the love of Pete, I hope the school doesn't call due to a sick or hurt kid. Irrational fear takes over. I had better cut my errands short and get back home.

Then it hits me — I am an ADDICT. Thinking that this could be a blog post, I look for my phone to write a note. Dang. Maybe I can leave myself a voice mail message. Duh, no.

Upon returning home, I see my lonely phone on the counter. I run to it like a long lost lover. As I pick it up, a wave of relief comes over me. This is a problem. I should be able to function without my phone, right? Something needs to be done. So, thinking there may be others with an affliction similar to my own, I developed this 8 step program. If you know someone who is in need, turn the page, read, copy, and send.

8 Steps to Overcoming iAddiction:

1. Admit you have a problem (isn't that always number one?).

2. Break up your day with "Tech Time Outs." Get off the grid and be free.

3. Silence your phone when working on an important task.

4. Engage with people, making the conversation a priority (not the phone).

5. Safety first when driving. Phones truly are a dangerous distraction.

6. Build a technology tower. Pile all the phones up and the first to check pays the check.

7. Wait and watch. Create a "No Phone Zone." Maybe it's the dinner table. Maybe it's at Grandma's house. Use "Head-Up" time to observe and be in the moment.

8. Trust that it is okay to just "be" rather than always having to have something to "do."

Start slow and see what transpires. Without my face in my phone at the UPS Store, I became aware of a man lugging big boxes and was able to run to the door and help. Having a phone-free drive gives you time to think — and is the right thing to do. Waiting in lines sans phone will give you an opportunity to connect with people (what a concept!). I mean, what did we do before smart phones? That's right — we survived.

And yes, I did go back to UPS and take that photo.

Procrastinate Later

As I look around my office, I see the land of unfinished projects: kid's artwork meant for scrapbooks, client files stationed on my desk to remind me to send a special thank you note, info from conferences waiting for action, and randomness that needs to be filed (but should be tossed instead).

Do you live on SOMEDAY ISLE too? Someday, I'll have time to make those special memory books. Someday, I'll purge the paper that I don't need. Someday, I'll tackle my "that would be nice to do" list. Of course, all of this hinges on the dreaded phrase, "When I have time!"

Suddenly, it hit me — I'm waiting for time that really doesn't exist. Phantom Time. That is, time that will always be replaced with more important tasks. Always.

However, it is not a lost cause. We can do some things to jump-start into action:

GET THE URGE TO PURGE

Learn to let go. Take one drawer, one kitchen cabinet, or one office cubby that makes you loco. Set a timer for 20 minutes and go to town. Be tough on yourself. Do you *really* need this? If you haven't touched an item recently, maybe it isn't that important. It's like when you get ready to move, and you realize that you haven't unpacked boxes from your previous move. Years have passed and obviously, you haven't missed the contents. Sell, recycle, donate — it feels great!

HOT TIP

Marry like items (office supplies, gift wrap) so you can live in peace and harmony.

YOU'VE GOT TO MOVE IT MOVE IT MOVE IT
There's a line from the kids movie, Madagascar, "You've got to MOVE IT MOVE IT MOVE IT." *You really do have to move it!* Don't just shuffle things from one side of your desk to the other. Get rid of clutter piles. Take action. Do it. Delegate it. Or dump it.

TAKE A PICTURE — IT WILL LAST LONGER
Who says you must keep every art project your kids create? Take pictures and get a photo book from one of those photo book builder sites. What will your kids do with a box of their handprints and macaroni sculptures when they are adults? A book takes up less space, collects less dust, and is far easier to enjoy.

FEEL THE FEAR AND DO IT ANYWAY
Fear prevents us from doing so many things. Just take a baby step. Make the call. Send that e-mail. Apply for that job! What do you have to lose???? If you don't succeed at the very least you've learned what NOT to do!

GO SET READY
Okay, make the decision to **GO** for your goal. **SET** a time and space. Get **READY** to release yourself from the guilt. Escape from *SOMEDAY ISLE*. Don't procrastinate today — do that later. Give yourself a break, and beware of Phantom Time. The time is now. Let's go!

Break Up, Shake Up, Wake Up

You may have heard the term, *Conscious Uncoupling* regarding the regarding the break-up of a celeb couple. Ahhh, the joy of semantics. My eye roll also got me thinking about the end of relationships — both personally and professionally. Maybe we could all use more *Conscious Uncoupling* in our lives. Is it a bad thing? Sad thing? Maybe it's a really good thing!

Have you ever been in a friendship that was totally exhausting? You go for dinner with this "friend" and return home only to feel beaten-up and drained? Have you ever wondered why you return to the same dry cleaner — the one who has scorched seven of your best shirts?

But how can you break up? All that history! You may feel that you have been together for so long that you can't — you went to third grade together! You were in each others' weddings! This is your golf buddy! Or maybe, it's the accountant who's been doing your taxes for 30 years?

Wait! Did you know that maintaining any of these relationships is not required? It is **voluntary**.

KNOW WHEN TO SAY NO... MORE

Friendship is a precious thing. So too are solid relationships with doctors, bankers, pet sitters, and manicurists. Connections with people who lift you up are nourishing and rewarding. Connecting with those who drag you down is exhausting! Determine how you feel most of the time during these interactions. If the relationship always leaves you feeling drained, perhaps it is time to move on. "Save the Drama for your Mama!"

CONFRONTATION? YIKES!

Deep down you know what to say and do. You have two clear choices: you can be honest or simply avoid the person completely. If you take the more direct approach, make sure to use "I" language. *"Right now I need to spend more time with my family."* Or, *"I think I need to take a break."* Heck, you don't have to explain anything if you don't want to. Just make sure you leave the other person with ego intact. Be kind. Be caring. Send the person off with love and good wishes.

WHAT'S NEXT?

Understand that you have the power to choose who you want to be with in your life. Releasing those negative people opens the door for new and better relationships. Don't feel guilty. Relationships evolve. Time is precious. Be a best friend to yourself and decide to do some *Conscious Uncoupling*. **Unless it is with me… I will try to do better. I love you. Truly. Don't leave me.**

It's YOUR Business

3

Surviving Those Fast Balls

Say Yes to Saying NO

Does doing everything for everyone make you cranky?

Do you often say Yes to things when you really mean NO?

Have you ever overheard someone say that they can't say NO?

Take control of your overscheduled day by using one simple word — NO. Don't worry, you can say the word NO — you just choose not to, due to pangs of guilt, obligation, or not wanting to hurt feelings. **Consider this: when you say NO to something, you are saying YES to something else** — your family, your health, or maybe your SANITY?

Here's the skinny — we only have so many hours in the day, and we usually sacrifice spending time on what really matters for time spent doing a bunch of insignificant stuff that really doesn't. **Most of us are not victims; we're volunteers!** Hey, if you organized the company holiday party the last FIVE years, stop being selfish and let someone else have the opportunity. If you have been the soccer coach for the last three seasons, give another dad a chance already! Don't get me wrong, if you dig these things, that's great, but no whining about it when you are so busy that your own dog growls at you when you walk through the door.

If it is a request of a personal nature, try saying NO without a lengthy explanation. Skip the excuses and take charge of your time. Keep in mind that you are not rejecting the person, just the request. It may take practice to say NO, but once you get through it and realize the earth hasn't stopped rotating, you gain confidence saying NO in the future.

If you still don't think you can use the word NO, here is the stealth CIA-Easy-Way-to-Say-NO without even having to use the word:

C - Clarify. Play back the request, "You would like me to make copies?"

I - Inform. Explain what you are currently working on, "Right now I'm working on the end of the month report."

A - Alternative. Offer alternatives making the one that includes you the least desirable. "I would be happy to make those copies first thing tomorrow morning, or you may want to do them yourself if you need them faster."

Now, do NOT CIA your boss — you may end up MIA. If it is a boss request, try this, "I would be happy to do XYZ for you. What project from this morning would you like me put on the back burner?"

Give it a try. NO? Oh, I see you are practicing already — good for you!

What if You Don't Have an Emergency Escape Slide?

Once upon a time, a flight attendant performed a wild job exit via escape slide. Why did this act of defiance capture the imagination of the entire country? Are you kidding?! Who hasn't dreamt of leaving a "job from hell" in a really dramatic fashion — especially those who work with the ever-entitled public!

I'm flashing back to my college summer job at Walt Disney World. I worked on the *It's a Small World* attraction **[insert 'It's a Small World' song here].** Well, one of the rotations was stroller control — probably the *most unhappy* job at the "happiest place in the world." Families would drop off strollers in an assigned area and cast members (code for employees) had to create order out of stroller chaos. A fellow worker placed a sign on the employee side of a secret entrance that read, *"Welcome to Stroller Hell."* While posting that little sign must've felt fabulous, it was not looked upon favorably by Mickey, and the employee was promptly fired.

DAMN THOSE CONSEQUENCES

A cartoon in the *Dallas Morning News* had the flight attendant landing at the bottom of the slide, only to find himself at the end of the unemployment line. Although we can dream, acting on our frustrations

Before You Deploy the Emergency Slide, Try One of These Ideas...

- Ask for help when you need it.
- Create a smile file. Include cards, happy letters, cartoons, and stories that can shift your mood positively.
- Surround yourself with funny friends.
- Journal out your anger and then rip the paper to shreds.
- Change the scene: take your lunch to the park instead of the breakroom, go on a coffee run, or hit the stairs two at a time.

Surviving Those Fast Balls | It's YOUR Business

could lead to bad consequences, or in the case of the frustrated flight attendant, a reality show. Both are remarkably unappealing to most people.

WHY CAN'T EVERYONE JUST GET ALONG?

There's a Facebook group called, "Be kinder than necessary, because everyone you meet is fighting some sort of battle." You never know what people are going through that makes them behave the way they do. Learning to handle the small stressful moments in your life will help you manage the big stressful ones better. Before you SNAP **[insert 'Take This Job and Shove It' song],** take a moment to breathe, make up a story about the annoying person's past and daydream about deploying the emergency slide — without acting on it! You may not love your job, but hey, a paycheck is a good thing.

Overshare Beware

TOO MUCH INFO?

As a motivational speaker, I try to be uplifting and inspirational. But it's hard sometimes because people can be oblivious. Have you ever had someone corner you — someone you hardly know — and blather on, telling you his deepest, darkest secrets. Clearly the expectation is that you'll sit like a bobble-head doll, continuously nodding, and quietly listening. What?!

FAIRWAY ADVENTURE

My mom called me the other day frustrated with a fellow golfer. She had become a victim of the OVERSHARE. "It was as if he was applying for a job. I know EVERYTHING about this man. He is a vet, has a purple heart, does 100 sit-ups every night, and he's in love with his Golden Doodle named Snickers." Between golf shots he would come over to her cart and give her another piece of "this is my life." He never once asked her anything, or even gave her a chance to respond to his life story. She started to hit the ball to opposite sides of the fairway to get some peace and quiet.

THE ME MONSTER

Not only is oversharing uncomfortable, it is frustrating because it usually leads to under-listening, eye-rolling, and that urge to blurt out, "Don't you wanna know ANYTHING about me?!"

But TMIers never ask reciprocal questions. Have you ever had this happen? While minding your own business waiting at the doctor's office, you say hello to someone and what she hears is, "Let me tell you why I am here!" [showing you her scar]. After a long diatribe, the person then sits back, puts her head in a magazine and leaves you dumbfounded. I recently had a grocery store clerk comment on my cart contents and then tell me about her lazy husband. Cue the awkward silence.

AN ESCAPE PLAN

It is tough because people mistake oversharing as a shortcut to bonding. Know this... typically oversharing is not a way to instant intimacy. Rather, it's simply inappropriate self-indulgence. You may have experienced this in person or have seen it on social media? People, Facebook is not your diary!

HERE'S HOW TO HANDLE THE ONE-WAY CONVO:

- **The Honest Reply:** *Wow, that is a lot of personal information, and I'm not sure how to respond.*

- **The Empathetic Switch:** *That's too bad. Can you believe how quickly February is going by?*

- **The Block:** For online repeat TMI offenders, you can always block their posts (they won't know) or in extreme cases, hit the "unfriend" button.

- **The Mirror:** Make sure you are not the perp. Whether in person or on social media, TMI is just that... TOO MUCH INFORMATION and trust me when I say, no one wants to hear about your sinus infection, sex life (okay, maybe), or see a picture of your ingrown toenail (excuse me while I vomit).

Keep this in mind... **Venting can be healthy — within reason.** Consider words like *dialogue and conversation* (this happens when multiple parties participate in an interchange). Remember that saying too much or the wrong things can undermine your relationships, career, and business. Beware of the overshare, and when in doubt, leave it out. Oops, did I say too much?

HOT TIP

Try your best to be more *interested*, than *interesting*.

Mean People Suck
(energy, profits, and your bottom line)

When did people stop having fun in their jobs? Granted, I know not every job is "fun," but turn that frown upside down, Grumpy Pants. Global Whining is at epidemic proportions. Don't add to it! If you can add play into your work, you may find that people like to work with you, customers are happier, and a better bottom line is the result.

As a professional speaker, I travel... a lot. By now, you'd think I had perfected it. Not so. With nearly three million miles on American, I still travel like a rookie. It is not unusual for me to haphazardly pack the morning of a trip, leave late and have to sprint through the airport while saying a prayer for a short security line. Shake your head if you will — I shake my head enough for both of us — but it is sort of S.O.P. for me. On a recent multi-city trip, I missed the cut-off to check my bag (full of books) by two minutes.

Global Whiner/Ticket Agent: "You're late."

Me: "I know... is there anyth-"

GW/TA: "Shhh... don't say a word and I will try to help you." Mumble, mumble, mumble, something about people needing to be quiet, plan better, mumble, mumble, mumble.

After running back and forth behind the counter and hitting 10,000 keystrokes, she checked my bag, and curtly handed me a boarding pass, (insert mean-spirited voice) "I am the only one who would have done this for you. You'd better run." I felt like a beaten puppy. Bad Traveler — BAD!

Yes, I was grateful she helped me make my flight, and sure she had the 'right' to judge me (whatever that means), but making me feel small didn't make me love the airline more. Au contraire.

THE SHAME GAME

Have you ever gotten what you wanted only to feel yucky inside? Have you screwed up only to have someone keep reminding you that you are a dork... especially someone you are giving your business/money to? It feels wrong.

Trying to do too much the morning I left for the airport was totally my fault. But instead of making my morning worse, the agent could have brightened it! Simple words such as, "Let me help you. I will do what I can. Hang tight." Anything but trying

Surviving Those Fast Balls | It's YOUR Business

to shame me into gratitude (not possible, by the way). What a gift a little understanding would have been, and it would have increased the loyalty of this 3 Million Mile Super Triple Platinum Diamond Travel-More-Than-Pilots customer. I would have walked away singing her praises, feeling grateful, and promoting her airline to anyone who would listen.

Obviously, we can't control others. But, if you're the one having one of those days and the mean monster awakens within you, try some of these...

Go for the Oscar. Check your troubles and bad attitude at the door. How would you act if you loved your job and the people you worked with? Pretend you do and see how it turns your day around.

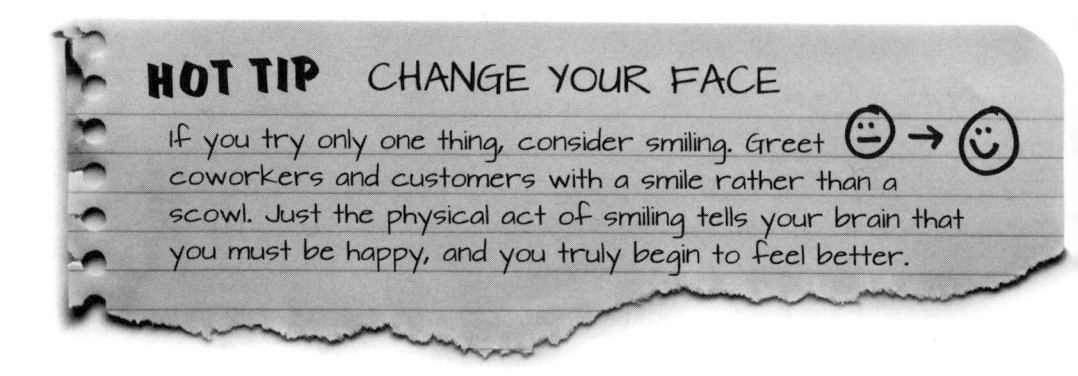

> **HOT TIP   CHANGE YOUR FACE**
>
> If you try only one thing, consider smiling. Greet coworkers and customers with a smile rather than a scowl. Just the physical act of smiling tells your brain that you must be happy, and you truly begin to feel better.

Wash out your mouth. Take the positive words challenge. See if you can go a day without saying anything negative. No gossip, criticizing, or judging allowed. Only allow positive words to come out of your mouth. You will be surprised at how good that tastes.

BOOGIE - **B**e **O**utstanding **O**r **G**et **I**nvolved **E**lsewhere. Get out! There are so many people out there who don't have jobs, who would absolutely LOVE the job you are griping about. If you don't like your job and you're sure you never will, find something else, and move over. You're taking up space in someone else's dream job.

And if you are on the receiving end of a Global Whiner one day, make up a story about that person — *why is she acting this way* — and move on. In the case of my GW, maybe her computer's omnectivicator just broke. Or maybe she just found out she's responsible to save the planet from an incoming piece of space junk. It could happen.

Remember: don't just live for the weekends! You spend too much time at work to be miserable. Learn to like it or even *gasp* LOVE it. Watch employee tension decrease and employee retention increase. You'll have happier customers and a better bottom line.

And, don't be late for your flight, but if you are, go easy on yourself. You may be the only one.

70 | www.ChristineCashen.com

LET IT GO (not just a catchy movie tune!)

Oh, how I wish I could belt out a tune like Idina Menzel in Disney's *Frozen*. Well, I can belt it out, but the dogs in the neighborhood howl wildly. No worries. I don't let my lack of singing skills stop me with this song. It is just too perfect. Let It Go. Many of us need a song like this as a stress mantra.

When your anger is triggered, it is hard to think logically. Having a mantra such as "Let It Go," or one of your choosing can save the day. But alas, the words don't always work! So, make up your own to fit the bill.

It happened just the other day. My son could not get over something my daughter did, so I began singing *Let it Go* and made up my lyrics:

Let it go

Let it go

I'm one with peace and calmmmm

Let it go

Let it goooooo

I love being your mommmmm

Here I stand and here I'll stayyyy

Let the fight rage on

Your fighting never bothered me anyway!

Yup, you have no idea how many songs I have ruined for my kids this way.

A theme song may come in handy when:

- You get worked up over something trivial
- You come across something you have no control over
- Someone breaks one of your pet peeve rules
- Your partner/spouse does something to annoy you
- You're about to explode

Have you heard this Disney song so many times from your kids that you find IT is the trigger for your anger?!? Find the perfect song for you! Is it Survivor's, *Eye of the Tiger?* Pharrell's *Happy*? Katy Perry's, *Roar?* Frank Sinatra's, *My Way?* Sing it loud and proud and **LET IT GO!**

Facebook Face-Off: Should a Smackdown be a PDA? (Public Display of Aggression)

Have you ever seen or been a part of an angry war of words on Facebook? Have you ever seen a response to a post that made you cringe?

Until recently, I'd been only a silent observer on the sidelines of such uncomfortable exchanges. But no more! Just last week, my innocent comment resulted in a somewhat heated exchange, and then my "friend" said he was going to "delete." Delete? The comment? The Facebook connection? Our friendship?

WHY AM I HERE?

OMG! It seems as though people have forgotten the concept of friendship. With the click of a button, you can un-friend someone. It really is as simple as that. Although sometimes we all might wish it were that easy, real life friendships don't work that way.

Surviving Those Fast Balls | *It's YOUR Business*

The whole purpose of being a part of this online community is to connect at a rapid pace with numerous friends simultaneously. What I love about Facebook is the ability to build on a friendship that you wouldn't normally be able to, due to distance or time.

So what to do when someone makes a truly bone-headed comment? While your first inclination may be to pound a heated response into your keyboard and hammer down the send button, firing off a brilliant message for all to see, there are really no winners in the PDA world.

WHY CAN'T EVERYONE JUST GET ALONG?!

What you post says a lot about you, whether in your status or your comments. It is awesome when my mom declares, "You have some really great friends. I love reading your wall because they are so supportive… and funny!" Yes, I'm fortunate to have some pretty cool, funny and talented friends — not to mention, kind, loving, and supportive. There aren't any "haters" in my circle — that I'm aware of anyway. They are more into public displays of affection than aggression. That's the way it should be. Peace out.

Prevent a Facebook Face-Off:

- Stick with people you truly know on your friend list. It's not about the numbers. Quality, not quantity, right?
- If you don't agree with something, consider taking it to your local Inbox instead of waving your dirty laundry in public. If you are having a fight at Christmas dinner, you would take it to another room, right? Same thing with Facebook.
- Pick up the phone. Find out what the other person is thinking. Tone is everything.
- Remember the saying, "It takes two to tango?" Consider walking away. Delete the comment and go for a walk.
- People can interpret written words any which way. Sometimes, a smiley face isn't enough to take the sting off a biting comment. It reminds me of the backhanded, "Bless Your Heart," one may get down South. Consider alternative interpretations!
- Remember why you joined Facebook in the first place — to connect and reconnect in a positive way.
- And most important, remember what your mama said, "If you don't have anything nice...."

It's YOUR Business

4

Living in the Moment

Are We There Yet?

On our car trip in Michigan this summer, it wasn't long before the kids started asking the universal car question... *"Are we there yet??"*

Knowing we still had a long way to go, I had to quash this line of questioning straight away. *"Yes, we are exactly where we need to be."* This bought us a little bit of silence as they tried to figure out what I was saying. That was my answer the next time as well. They stopped asking.

As annoying as *Are we there yet?* is when my kids ask it again and again, I've found that many adults ask that question throughout their lives. Am I there yet? I will be *there* when I graduate from college, get a job, get married, have kids, when kids move out, change my job, make X number of dollars, retire, etc. Too many of us wait for a certain event to happen before we believe we'll reach our destination of happiness and contentment.

STOP.
You are exactly where you are. If you don't like where you are now, think like a GPS: recalculate and change direction. But whatever you do, take time to enjoy the journey. You've probably heard the saying, **Wherever you go... there you are. And you are. Enjoy.**

Digitally Distracted

I was speaking at an event recently and the organizers were having a drawing after my program. Before I got on stage, the emcee had some remarks, then announced the drawing. He kept repeating, "You must be present to win!" over and over. It was as if the clouds parted and the angels were singing... *"ahhhhhhhhh be present to win."* There is more to that statement than we realize. It is the gift of our attention. Be present to win.

ATTENTION!

We aren't always present these days. In order to stay ahead and be productive, many of us are multitasking constantly. It is typical to see a dad at a sporting event spending all of his time looking down at his phone, rather than at the field. Or, I often see a group of women on a "girls night out" evening, phones in hand, spending more time checking in on their phones rather checking in with their friends. I remember taking my children to have lunch with another mom and her

Living in the Moment | It's YOUR Business | 79

children. Her kids were playing video games, while my kids were coloring with the restaurant crayons and placemats. It made me sad to see the lack of connection and communication between the children. It was like we weren't there at all. Are we starting kids on the wrong path?

> **HOT TIP**
> Stop checking. Start doing!

TWITTER NOT

We are all digitally distracted. Has it become passé to single-task? Can we do it anymore? A good friend of mine gave up social media for Lent. She said it was difficult in the beginning, but then she was amazed at all the extra time she had. For me, I needed to post a note on my computer screen, "stop checking and start doing." When I was stuck or faced with an undesirable task, I would turn to a social networking site and waste time, using it as a procrastination tool. Why do I feel it is necessary to follow every little mundane move of others? Why do I feel the need to post my own? Okay, it can be a great way to connect with people from the past and it is a quick and easy way to keep in touch — without really taking the time to keep in touch (is that really a good thing?), but we need to set limits.

YO BRO

My brother is a super busy guy. He owns restaurants and a microbrewery and is super-involved in civic activities in his town. He is not easy to connect with, so when he suggested we use Skype to better stay in touch, I jumped on it. We just had our first conversation and I felt strange because all I could do was talk to him. What I mean by that is that I wasn't typing an e-mail, watching TV, cleaning, or folding laundry — I was solely focused on him. It has been awhile since I have had a conversation like that. It was good.

GIVE IT ALL TO ME!

Halfway through convos with my mom, she will say, "I can hear you typing," and in turn I tell her that I know she is in the middle of a TV show due to her lack of response. How does it make you feel knowing you have a fraction of someone's attention? Not good. We need to be present to win in our relationships. It won't be easy, but I'm going to work on it.

Living in the Moment | *It's YOUR Business* | 81

Let's Digitally Downsize:

- When my kids/significant other come into my office, I will turn away from the computer and give them my full attention.

- Over the weekend, I will limit computer time and be present with my family.

- When out with friends, I'm making a pact to limit phone/text usage.

- When my partner is talking to me, I will not pull out my cell phone even when it "stuns" me.

- I will cut back to checking social networking sites to only 2x a day and limit my time on them.

- Manage Incoming Traffic — If you don't know how, find a 12-year-old who can help you set-up your phone so you are only getting notifications that are truly important.

My name is Christine Cashen and I am digitally distracted. I know admitting it is the first step to recovery. You've got to start somewhere! Signing off now and I hope you do the same.

Facebook Envy

Love you Facebook — CURSE you Facebook.

Have you ever read your Facebook news feed and felt a pang of jealousy, compared yourself with others, or felt as though everyone is having more fun than you?

Don't get me wrong, I love getting a glimpse into my friends' lives. And know this: I'm pretty happy, content, and grateful. But, I'm also human, petty, and flawed! Can we all just get real here for a minute? Yes, I do want to spend every moment with my beautiful children, have cocktails every afternoon with my gal-pals, travel to the most exotic locales, AND have time to go see the Rolling Stones in Mexico City. But I can't. And when you can, it makes me a little jealous. Check out some of these folks who have given me that twinge of FB envy. Maybe you've had it too?

Grass is always greener on the other side of a FB post.

Margarita Moms — What the heck are my mom friends doing meeting for margaritas in the middle of the afternoon? Yes, I work and am jealous. However, I also think I would have to take an afternoon nap, instead of taking care of my kids, if I had a mid-day cocktail. It is tough to admit, but after judging these moms, I'm back to being envious.

Business Booms — Looking at my speaker friends presenting in front of huge audiences in amazing places gives me a tiny pang of envy. Sure, I'm busy as I want to be, but seeing pix of them behind podiums at the Bellagio in Vegas makes me feel inadequate — especially if I'm off the road for a week and getting on my family's nerves.

Time Takers — I'm envious of those who have a lot of time. "Just got up and it is already noon!" and "Totally relaxed and back from a 5-day spa retreat!" My husband argues that getting off FB would create a windfall of time. He is right of course. But, the voyeur and extrovert in me will not give FB up. Plus, extra time usually gets filled up with house cleaning — not a spa trip.

Thrillers — It's wonderful to see pictures of friends hiking the Himalayas, but it stings a little to see these posts, having just returned home from a dog walk, plastic bag with dog poop, in hand.

Also in the thrillers category are my Harley-riding friends. It does make me happy to think of them on their rally of rebels, riding with the wind in their hair and leather on their backs. However, it does lead to a big bummer when I get in my scratched-up mini-van to go pick up the kids. Dang, I knew we should have gotten the sun roof!

Vacationers — Ahhh Aruba, Hawaii, Belize... I must say I do enjoy seeing your pictures and yes, wishing I were there. Thoughts of your sandy tropical toes were running through my mind, while I was picking marshmallow out of my hair at a recent scouting event.

REACTION? TAKE ACTION!

Well, well, well. After all is read and done on FB, I realize that I shouldn't be having a *reaction* to all of this — instead I need to take some *action!*

Vacation rocks! Wish you were here – LOL!

There is no reason I can't spice up my own existence. There's no reason you can't either! Call your tribe and schedule an early afternoon cocktail. Take charge of your career! Get off your bottom and plan a romantic dinner at that bistro you've been wanting to try. As a fellow tennis player once told me while we were playing, "Tennis is not a spectator sport." Neither is life.

The Fountain of Texting Truth

So, one day you're texting someone in the mall. The next day you're featured in a viral video on YouTube. And the next, you're on *Good Morning America*. How could this be, you ask?

A few years ago, a woman was casually walking through a mall and got so wrapped up in texting that she fell into the fountain. The misstep was captured on the mall security camera and subsequently posted on YouTube, quickly garnering over 3 million hits.

It doesn't end there. The security guard who leaked the footage was fired. And the woman, who we will call Cathy (because that's her name) hired a lawyer.

Lawyer: "We certainly plan to hold any and all people responsible."

Me: "Are you kidding me?" Responsible? Cathy, perhaps you should look in the mirror. Were you expecting mall security to hold your hand while you were walking through the mall texting? Or maybe, a guard rail around the fountain? Oh yeah… alert the jury! Cathy actually works in the MALL?! Huh?!"

But wait! I've just learned that Cathy has bigger problems than being publicly humiliated, as she is facing 5 felony counts of theft for stealing a co-worker's credit card and going charge happy. BTW, she says she was texting a "church friend" before the fall. Do you think it was about the felony charges? I digress....

LOL!

Here's the deal. First off, circumstances would be very different for our *splasher* had she not come forward, because I doubt anyone would have recognized her from the grainy video. Things also would be different if she had not come out and said that the video was not funny. Not funny? Did she see the footage??? Come out and LAUGH about it with all of us.

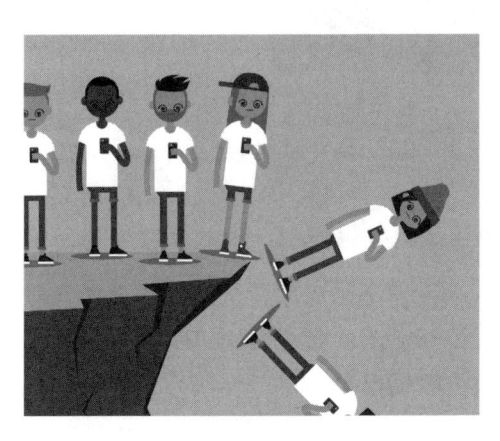

TEXTING TIPPING POINT

Cathy could be the new spokesperson for the dangers of **Texting While Walking (TWW)**. Come on, now is your chance to put on your big girl bloomers and call out those other mindless texters who may be at risk! Tell them about the dangers and that there is in fact life after falling in a fountain. Think of those poor souls who are, right this very minute, hunched over, typing away, risking their lives crossing the street, ricocheting off various stationary sidewalk objects, and bumping into other unsuspecting pedestrians.

LAWYER BE GONE!

Cathy — I know you can change all this... help others learn from your mistakes. How about "TA" — "Texters Anonymous?" Look at your fountain bath as a baptism. Do something for the betterment of humanity. You Cathy, and you alone, can make a difference. Take a stab at making the world a better place — one lonely walking texter / distracted-driver at a time! All of us need a reminder to pay attention to the world and not just our phones.

Who Made Downtime a Crime?

Are you burned out on GOALS? Does the thought of a New Year's Resolution give you hives? Have you ever just wanted to kick back for an entire day with NOTHING required of you — a totally free day! You are in luck. We're not talking about goals here. We're talking about freedom, balance, and less pressure.

Here's the deal. I don't know about you, but after the hubbub of running a household, running a business, and running around after my family — I am wiped out. I don't want to run a marathon. I don't want to learn to (name the fad here). I want to run to my bed and get into the fetal position.

Downtime does not equal slacker.
Give up the guilt!

TIME AFTER TIME

When January 1 hits, there is always a ton of pressure to set goals and get a move-on. I say WAIT! Don't get me wrong, I think goals are wildly important. I also think timing is everything. I am going to kick-off my New Year February 1 because I am just not ready to dive into productivity quite yet. That is probably perfect timing because I will be well rested and back into the routine. Plus, the gym starts to clear out.

Downtime does not equal slacker (unless you never get into gear). You shouldn't feel guilty for wearing your jammies past noon. Don't regret curling up on the couch with a good book. Binge watching a series on Netflix does not make you a loser. Who made downtime a crime?!? Give up the guilt! Downtime has value. A friend recently said, "How is it possible that I'm already BEHIND! What?!? Give yourself a break. We need some time to just relax. Don't just look at the first day of the year as your big opportunity. Every *month* is a new start. Every *day* is a new start.

Some of us need **downtime before GO time.**

Give yourself permission to **just BE** for now.

Start your engines... when you are **good and READY.**

Done is Better Than Perfect

I have a neighbor who is a compulsive leaf blower. Maybe it's some manly attraction to power tools, but seriously, every day that *a leaf* falls (I really am serious), he's out sweeping, blowing, and literally picking leaves up, one-at-a-time, by hand.

DONE. DONE. DONE. DONE!

He probably considers us giant slackers — waiting for most leaves to fall before we start. I even like to leave a few. Don't they biodegrade and fertilize the yard? Truth be told, I don't think the average person doing a drive-by would notice that his A+++ yard looks any better than our solid B (unless they're on hands-and-knees, counting foliage)!

SAY CHEESE

Now let's talk about the family calendar. Every year I try to find THE perfect pictures. Will my sister-in-law think she looks bad? Is this the only picture I have of my nephew? So, I wait and wait, and get completely stressed. Sure, I have 300+ pictures to choose from, so why is finding 12 so tough? My engineer "voice of reason" husband calmly tells me each year — that if the calendars don't arrive until January 1, the family will still love them.

And then there are the holidays. I am in full panic mode. Cards to create, teacher gifts to buy, long distance gifts awaiting shipment, and every night I sit bolt upright at 1:00 a.m., because I've forgotten to move the frickin' Elf on a Shelf. Wait, not only do you have to move the Elf, you also need to find something creative for him to be doing!?

Here's a new one — I recently updated my logo and spent an inordinate amount of time deciding on the color. I mean, a lot of time. I'm not kidding here. I had 37 color variations to choose from, and not only did I spend far too much time on this myself — I also engaged every breathing human I could find to give me an opinion. Am I *not* going to get hired if I use a gradient? I think not. Wow, I hope not.

MADNESS

Bottom line here is that everyone's idea of DONE is a bit different. Of course, there is that distinction between DONE and DONE RIGHT. But we all know that some people take this to extremes. Is it time to ask yourself what your "DONE" is really about? I honestly think my leaf guy wants to get out of his house. Then there are those people who need to one-up others. And the Procrastinators — those who get heavily involved in something, to avoid something else. Then there's plain old OCD (there are good meds for this, btw).

In stressful times, DONE IS BETTER THAN PERFECT. This does not apply to bridge builders and brain surgeons, as well as others who are responsible for wildly important tasks. This is for those of us who put undue pressure on ourselves over trivial matters.

PERFECTLY IMPERFECT

Time for a wake-up call. It's easy to get sucked into the minutiae. Join me in shifting your perspective. They say, "Don't sweat the small stuff" and it's true! Done is better than perfect. Store bought pies. A few leaves in the yard. Calendars with average pictures. A book with a few typos — even after seven intelligent proof readers. It's all good.

Give yourself the gift of imperfection. Most likely, you'll be the only one who notices.

I Met Train on a Plane

How often do we sit on a plane — or anywhere for that matter — in our own zones, unaware of those around us? Whether it be a subway, plane, grocery store, or dentist's office, we are all thrust into the presence of others. Are you on your phone or just lost in your own thoughts? Are you truly present where you are?

WE'RE WITH THE BAND

On a recent flight to Orlando, I was with my speaker buddy, and we were lucky enough to be riding in the First Class section (thank you upgrade coupons). After 20 minutes of snappy banter, my friend looked at me and said, "Those dudes across the aisle are in a band." How could he know this? "They are wearing skinny jeans and hearing aids." Nice observation.

"Well, get the scoop," I implored. We discovered they were in the Grammy Award-winning band, Train. Cool. Hey, I've heard of them. They were big (as in popular) and cute (well okay... I couldn't really tell under the baseball caps and scruff).

Of course, we spent the rest of the flight using the Go-Go Flight internet service to watch YouTube videos and listen on our headphone splitters to all things Train.

As a former radio personality, I pride myself on being up on the music scene. I was surprised they sang *Drops of Jupiter*, *Meet Virginia*, and *Soul Sister*??? I thought that was Maroon Five! Wow, I guess it has been a long time since I have spun records... oh crap... now you see the problem.

BAGGAGE CLAIM STAKE OUT

When we landed, my friend had only carry-on luggage and went directly to the hotel. Happily, I had checked my bag so I had a legit reason to stalk Train into the baggage claim area. Come on, wouldn't you?! And of course I positioned myself right where the bags would be deposited. As hockey great, Wayne Gretsky once said, "A good hockey player plays where the puck is. A great hockey player plays where the puck is going to be." So, I positioned myself appropriately.

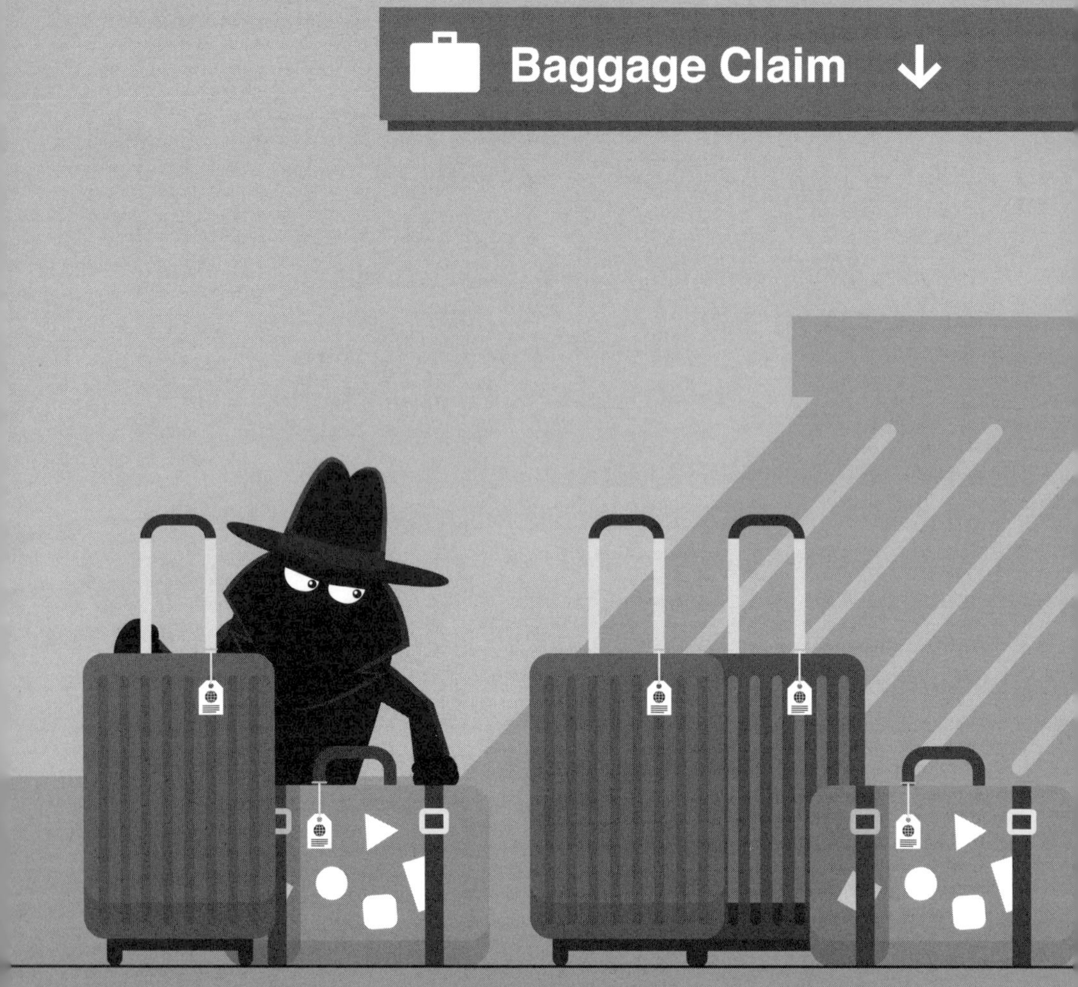
Baggage Claim

Using my crack investigative skills, I found out the roadie's name was Pergo, that the band was performing a local gig in Orlando, then moving on to Austria, then London. We did the requisite chit-chat and I learned that he is an avid reader. We swapped favorite book titles and he even said he would look up my book, *The Good Stuff,* on Kindle. (Really? You think?) As I was leaving baggage claim, I passed right by Pat Monahan, the lead singer of Train! "Have a great time in Austria!" I said casually and brushed by.

I'd truly planned to keep on going, but Pat had a smile the size of Texas and a twinkle in his eye. It stopped me in my tracks (Train tracks — sorry, I couldn't help myself). I backed up a few steps and said, "Can I get a photo opp?"

He was as gracious as he could be. "I'm really good at selfies," said Pat (to me!). I informed him that when I take selfies, all I see are chins. So, he grabbed my phone and captured the moment. OMG!

GET OUT OF YOUR ZONE

Thank goodness for my first-class friend — for lifting the virtual plane shades for me, so I could get some daylight and see what's going on in that big bad world!

Unfortunately, we are so programmed to stay in our own zones and not connect with others. Our faces are buried in our phones, catching up with people who are not there, while completely ignoring those who are. How much do we miss by not being present? How many really cool people are sitting right beside us and we overlook them because we're engaged in our own private Idahos?

Now you might not meet a Grammy Award-winning artist. It could be a person that you kinda know through "seven degrees of Kevin Bacon." Or maybe you meet the perfect new friend!

I met Train on a Plane. Lucky? Yes. Did I open myself up to my present surroundings?

Yes. Maybe you should too.

BUSY is a Four Letter Word

Everybody says they're busy. I've even said *"I'm crazy busy"* sometimes. But what does it really mean?

Are you lovin' your busy because your business is booming, your kids are soaring, and you've got this whole life balance thing under control? Might you even be bragging just a little (be honest with yourself here... I mean come on... who wants to admit that they're bored with life and not sure what direction to take... I digress). So, are you saying you're crazy busy because you want to paint a picture of your life for others as successful? Riding the tiger? On top of the world?

Or is your busy about whirlwind kid events, keeping up with bills, the "honey do" list, and trying to get a good night's sleep?

BUSY WITH?
Think hard about what your busy really means and what it is you want to communicate to others. But know this — no matter what your life is like, you DO have choices.

Don't use Busy as an excuse for not staying in touch... YOU get to choose, so make sure you make good choices here! Is your life rocketing by? People often say (when I say 'people,' I mean me), "Where is time going?!?" Who the heck knows? Every time I turn around I get a "due for a dental visit" postcard. Wasn't I just there last month? Six months seem to pass like six weeks. Are you with me on this? When a new season hits, it is always a surprise. Wasn't it just Christmas? Valentine's Day? July 4? Lunar eclipse? Back to school, Spring?

If you ever wonder where time is going, consider your wonder a gift. Just having the realization is key. The first step is admitting you have a problem, right? In that moment of clarity, STOP and evaluate whether you are in control of your time, or is your time controlling you?

CHECK THE TIME
The key is to look hard (really hard!) at how you're spending your time. Me? True confessions? I'm a Mashable/BuzzFeed junkie, which leads me to click on another story, then another... oh look, an article on 10 ways to avoid procrastinating! I'm a click bait marketer's dream.

Living in the Moment | *It's YOUR Business*

GUILTY AS CHARGED?

What about you? Are you watching *Law & Order* reruns from 2003 when you want to learn conversational French? Are you complaining that your boss doesn't appreciate you and wishing for a new job, but sending ZERO resumes out?

COMPLAIN DRAIN

Next time someone asks you what's new and you start into your rant about how busy you are, think about what you're really busy with! Everyone you talk to is busy. Stop complaining about being BUSY, stop it.

Just because you're busy, doesn't mean you're working on valuable things. Are you doing what matters to you? Why are you wasting time talking about it?

The next step? Decide to do something. Recognize and stop time thieves by becoming a time tamer. Do a quick priority check:

- Activate time limits for web surfing and social media. It is easy to click your way into a 3-hour time void. Stop checking. Start doing.

- Mark time for YOU on your calendar. Stop overscheduling (this goes for your kids too!) and actually schedule rejuvenators — exercise, meditation, and quiet time.

- Eliminate the YES SYNDROME — you can say NO more often.

- Remember to be in the moment — it truly is a present to be in the present.

HOT TIP:

Don't wait for time to slow down. It won't. Take charge today and tell time what time it is!

It's YOUR Business

Appreciat-cha!

5

Giving Thanks — the Right Way

A week before Thanksgiving, I asked my kids what they were thankful for and they replied, "Thanksgiving is not until next week." Huhhh? So, I had to whip out the, "We should be thankful everyday" speech. That got me thinking about thanking people, which led me to what bugs me about saying thanks and contemplating how we can do it better.

Here are some ways to make a thank you more meaningful and memorable:

NO SHAME IN A NAME

Thank you to the organizers. Thanks to those who helped me. Thanks to (insert large group). Does that really make anyone feel special? Drop the group thank you. By trying to include everyone, no one feels very special. Whenever possible, use names. Have you ever heard the saying, "The sweetest sound to anyone's ears is the sound of his own name."

BE SPECIFIC AND SINCERE

Hey man, thanks for everything. EVERY thing? What things? Tell the man what you appreciate in particular — the extra time he spent on that project, or the speedy service that she provided to the customer. Of course, be sincere in your appreciation. People can feel it!

Hey man, thanks for everything.

KEEP EMILY POST ALIVE

Thank you cards are an endangered species. If you're like me, you've wondered if some mailed gifts even made it to the recipient. It means so much and takes so little time to send a heartfelt thank you note. Go the e-mail route if you must, but phone calls and handwritten notes are always better, and more appreciated. Keep a blank set of cards at your desk, and your contacts handy. You might even consider doing a video thank you. Get a teenager to help you.

THE EYES HAVE IT

When you have the opportunity to thank someone, make sure to look that person in the eye. Direct eye contact deepens the message of gratitude and feeling of sincerity.

RESPOND APPROPRIATELY

When someone thanks you, a good response is *My Pleasure*, *Happy to Help*, or *You're Welcome*. Consider the underlying message that a phrase like *No Problem* sends. Are you saying it could have been a problem? Normally helping someone is a problem? Am I a problem? It may convey a sentiment you didn't intend.

DANKE MERCI **THANK** GRAZIE
GRACIAS **YOU** TACK
СПАСИБО OBRIGADO

SO, THANK YOU!

Dear (your name) — I know how busy you are with work and family, and I really appreciate your taking the time to read this book. If it makes you smile, I'd be grateful if you'd consider sharing these ideas. Thanks in advance! It means so much to me. Happy Thanksgiving (your name), I appreciate you more than you know.

You Can Ring My Bell... Or Not

A Kroger opened in our neighborhood. You've gotta love that new store smell and the fresh and perky employee attitudes. This store is awesome! It has a Sushi Bar, a Starbucks, and the Express Lanes have a sign that states, "*About* 15 items." Sweet! The pressure is off.

As usual, we are out of milk, cereal, and dog food. I'm on a fast grocery run between kid pick-up and 17 other errands. I approach the checkout and see that you can ring a bell for exceptional service. When you "ding," everyone yells, "WOOOOO!" I don't know why this cracks me up, but it does. So, I have been experimenting. If I ring the bell the moment I arrive

Appreciat-cha! | It's YOUR Business

at the cashier, does that ensure better service? If I don't ring the bell, do the checker and bagger feel disappointed? Do *I* get to yell, "WOOOOO!" or is it just for employees?

After many failed attempts at gathering any true intel, I decided to ask. Except, I may have asked the wrong cashier.

GETTING THE REAL SCOOP

"Excuse me, do you get happy when people ring the bell?"

"Not really."

"Really?!?"

"Well, I only like it when a manager is around to hear it. Mostly, it's just annoying."

This was a totally unexpected answer. Seriously? Doesn't everyone want their bell rung? (That doesn't sound right — but stick with the story). Doesn't everyone want to provide great service, whether a manager is around or not? If great service happens and a manager isn't around to witness it, did it actually take place?

WHAT THE BELL?

As a frequent bell ringer, I walked to my car downtrodden. It's like finding out there is no Easter Bunny or the real age of Mick Jagger. Sitting in the car, I thought about what just happened. There are some great lessons here:

- What you think motivates your employees, kids, bosses, partners... may not be what truly motivates them.

- Hire, surround yourself, and make friends with people who want the bell ringing.

- Check your own "WOOOOO!" Are you doing things that motivate others to want to ring your bell? Great service, attitude, professionalism?

- Are you ringing others' bells regardless of who is or is not watching?

TO RING OR NOT TO RING?

SO... Will I still ring the bell? Absolutely! If I truly get good service, the world should know! In this hectic life, there's still nothing like giving and getting a real, "WOOOOO!"

Go forth today, "WOOOOO" and be "WOOOOOed." Now more than ever we need more cheerleaders, fewer critics, and better customer service.

Appreciating Don

I want to tell you about Don, a truly wonderful guy. A great example of his wonderfulness (if that isn't a word, it should be) was the time he, his wife, and his mother-in-law were coming home from an overseas trip. He dropped them off curbside at the departure terminal and went on to return the rental car. It was super early and the place was still closed, so he threw the keys in the slot, left the car in the appointed spot, and shuttled back to the terminal.

The moment he stepped off the shuttle he realized that the luggage was still in the trunk of the car. Without making a fuss, he sent his wife and MIL on the original flight and bought a ticket on a much later flight so he could wait for the car rental place to open and fetch everyone's luggage. This was typical Don. No matter what happened, he always took it with great humor and sweet spirit.

UNEXPECTED GOOD BYE

Don just happens to be my father-in-law and he's on my mind today because this is the anniversary of his sudden and unexpected passing.

This time of year always makes me wonder... *Did he know how much I loved him?* Did he know how I'd so love to have his patience and kind spirit? (I heard him yell once in 15 years — at his dog. I yell at my kids and our danged dog 10x a day!) Does he know that I'm going to teach my kids — his grandchildren — to be just like him?

Think about it. Do the people closest to you truly know how much you appreciate them? Are there any "wrongs" between you and a family member or close friend that you need to make right? If something were to happen to that person *today*, would you be at peace?

SAY IT NOW

Don was a leader, volunteer, and mentor in his community for over 50 years. I remember when he and my mother-in-law came to visit for the last time. We created wonderful memories that I will forever cherish.

Pick up the phone today. Make time for those you love. Say you're sorry. And don't be shy with the *"I love yous."* It is not too late to appreciate. Rest in Peace, Papa Don.

**DON CASHEN
(1936 – 2012)**

When NO PROBLEM is a Problem

The waiter screwed up our order. I tell him that it is okay, and he responds with, "No problem." Ummm… it actually was a problem. Have you ever walked out of a store and said thank you and gotten the, "No problem" response? Did I miss a problem? When did everyone born after 1985 decide that "No problem" was interchangeable with "You're welcome?"

POR FAVOR

It shouldn't bother me, but it does, probably because I was born well before 1985. In my presentations, I often ask people about their pet peeves and this one comes up regularly, so I can't be alone in this thinking. Here's the deal — no problem reverses the terms of the transaction. Rather than you doing a favor for an establishment by shopping or eating there, now suddenly the establishment is doing you a favor by having its employees help you. Then they tell you that it was no big deal, seeing as how your server, associate, or whomever is getting paid to do that very thing (I think that's the definition of a "job," no?).

No problem is an appropriate response when telling someone you've gone out of your way to help — essentially communicating that the person shouldn't feel indebted. That is cool. But too often, hearing "no problem" when there is NOT a problem, causes a problem. I understand that the words, "You're welcome," may get tiresome, so let me offer a few alternate responses:

"My pleasure."   "Enjoy!"
"Certainly!"
"Thanks for coming in today!"
"Happy to help."
"SURE THING!"   "Thank YOU!"

It seems that "please" and "thank you" are becoming a lost art. And now we are losing "you're welcome"? I'm losing it along with my close vision. It is all too much.

Thank you for reading my rant. I hope you didn't just yell, "No problem!"

Are You a Conversation Killer?

You know the type — the people who command attention the entire conversation. You know everything about them and their day, yet they did not ask you ONE question in return! The interaction was more a monologue than a dialogue. Often times you walk away from these conversations and wonder why you feel frustrated. It is hard to change these people, so let's do a self-check on our skills.

GIDDY-UP

As a motivational speaker, people often ask questions about how I got started in the business and who my clients are, and I find myself getting giddy. Someone is interested in me! I have to relax and realize that they mostly want the cliff note version of my career path. It is fun to have an interesting job, but it is a conversation killer to wax on and on about it. I always try to steer the conversation back to them. Then they get to feel giddy, "Yippee, someone is interested in me!"

Let's constantly turn the conversation back to me

Appreciat-cha! | It's YOUR Business

THE ART OF SMALL TALK

The problem is that we all want to appear interesting, but true meaningful conversations occur when there is genuine interaction, where both parties converse equally and thoughtfully. The most important step is to be more interested in the other person than trying to be interesting to them. Yes, we want to bond and connect, but watch what happens when you are an engaged listener. Give others your full attention rather than waiting for them to take a breath, so you can hijack the conversation with something about yourself.

My engineer hubby is famous for this. When we are at parties, he will end up "talking" with someone and when I say talking, I mean that he listens, asks great questions and is truly present. People will then tell me what an amazing husband I have, which is funny because I know how my husband casts his spell — he is interested in them!

DOWN WITH THE ONE-UPPER

A subset of the conversation killer is the one-upper. You know people who, after listening to your story, have to top it with their story? Sometimes it becomes a contest of who had the worst day or who is the most stressed out or how many sporting events they had to sit through. Just let people have their moment. You're not performing or trying to win. I know it is hard, but if you beat them with an *even more embarrassing moment* (I always can), you've basically stolen the thunder and killed the conversation momentum. Don't be a banter bully.

THE BIG KEY

Do you want to have better and more meaningful connections and relationships?

Be aware of your conversation skills. Recognize when *you* are too long in the speaking spotlight. People have a story and they love when someone is interested in listening. Be present and pay attention to what others are saying. Ask questions. Make relating statements. Find a balance between listening and talking.

Converse.
Connect.
Engage.
Enjoy!

Stop Swatting and Say Thank You

You did a great job on the project!
Well, it was a group effort.

Your hair looks great!
Oh, I actually need a haircut.

I like your shirt.
This old thing? I've had it since high school.

> You are wicked smart!

> You look great!

> You rocked that meeting today!

I've done this... a lot lately. At a recent party, a colleague told me that I "always look cute," and I responded by telling her not to get any closer because with the excessive heat, I didn't smell that cute. It was an awkward moment for everyone within earshot. I felt terrible and she was clearly uncomfortable. What just happened? So much for my social skills.

SMACK BACK

Has this ever happened to you? You know — someone gives you a compliment and you swat it away? Or you give a quick compliment back to take the spotlight off you and prove the complimenter is in the wrong?

Why do we do this? To appear humble? Give me a break! If I say "thank you," will I really look like a conceited jerk? I think about golfing with my husband. When I tell him, "Great shot," he never responds with, "It was just lucky." He says *thanks*. And, it feels good for both of us.

GRACIOUS GETTING

A compliment is a gift. Lord knows we could all use more positivity in our lives, so why push it away? Could you see yourself rejecting a physical gift that someone handed you? Of course not! You wouldn't want to be rude to the gift giver, right? Right. You would say thank you and go on your way — even if it was a gift you didn't want or didn't think you deserved.

By accepting a compliment, you convey to the other person that you trust their judgment. So, next time you get one, instead of deflecting it, focus on receiving the compliment without judging the content. Practice saying, "THANK YOU" with a big smile, and accept the gift with grace. Trust me: everyone will be happier.

Give compliments freely. Accept them gratefully. As for me, next time I promise to keep the secret of my *Secret* not working, to myself.

Slam Dunk or Air Ball?

Have you ever noticed that there are some people you look forward to seeing? Knowing you'll be in their company puts a skip in your step and raises your spirits. Then there are others you dread seeing, knowing it's going to be an energy-zapper. Why is this the case? Because of how they make you feel when you are with them, and how they make you feel about yourself. I have some friends who are riding rainbows. They worship unicorns, wear kaleidoscope glasses, and are eternal optimists.

I have other friends who are constantly talking about their bad bosses, climate change, and politics. I love them all BUT, I enjoy my unicorn friends much more than my bad boss friends. Why?

Because I like feeling happy, optimistic, and joyful. Don't get me wrong. All of these topics are valid and interesting. My bad boss friends are wonderful people, but after I'm with them I feel sad, drained, and out of sorts.

GLOBETROTTERS RULE

We took the kids to see the Harlem Globetrotters – yes, they are still trotting around and just as much fun as I remember from my childhood. What I don't remember is being able to buy an expensive basketball and head down to the floor to get autographs from players.

After much begging from my son, we invest in a basketball. He's thrilled. Then we notice the mass of humanity heading out of the bleachers and down the stairs to the playing floor for autographs. Watching everyone jockeying for position, we realize this was a very bad idea.

Then, I had a good idea. I say to my son, "Hey, honey, why don't you head down and we will wait up here in the stands? We will watch you the whole time." Not a good idea. We watched our pensive son get pushed around, further and further from the players. I almost became a bleacher mom yelling from the stands, "Get in there! Use your elbows! Come on, ref!"

Appreciat-cha! | *It's YOUR Business* | 123

EPIPHANY

After much chaos and close monitoring, I see our son look over to the Globetrotters emcee in the corner, who only had a few autograph seekers. My telepathic senses kicked in as I wished he would go over there so he could get at least ONE signature. It worked! He walked over to the charismatic man with dreadlocks, wearing a sequined jacket. I see a spirited conversation between the two of them. After the signature and banter, my son turns around with a huge smile on his face and floats back up to our seats in the nosebleed section.

"What in the heck happened?!?" I enquired.

Our son replied, "I asked the emcee how he was doing and he said, 'I'm better because YOU are here!'"

Wow! This interchange clearly made an impression. Of course, the emcee probably used that line with everyone, but our son thought it was meant only for him. It made him feel truly special.

I tried this line with my favorite post office worker, Micah. He is always professional, patient, and kind. He asked me how I was and I told him I was better because he was there. Which was true. My reward was the most beautiful smile I have ever seen.

COMING AND GOING

There are just some people you are happier to see coming than going. The reverse is also true. There are people you are happier to see leave a room than enter it. Which one are you? When people leave an interaction with you, do they feel better or worse? Truly think about your energy in this world. We are more interconnected than we realize. I know I'm better because you are here, sweet reader. Thank you.

Thank you

Afterburner

It truly **is your business**... your work, your happiness, and your life. Do you wait for others to make your life better? Don't wait. Don't put it off. Don't "someday I will." Make bold and courageous choices, baby steps if you wish, but be a person of positive action. Do it now! You are the CEO of YOU.

There is plenty of darkness around us. We must be the light for ourselves and be an example for others. It is nice to have a good life, and it is better when others have a good life because of us. That starts with us leading the way. Regularly step out of your routine, gain confidence, and believe in your own capabilities. You will find out things about yourself that you didn't know. You have more power and control than you realize. No more blaming others, blaming your past, and waiting for opportunity to knock. Break down the door to new possibilities to be fulfilled and happy.

Choose to make a stand. Choose to make a difference. Choose to live the life you deserve.

Acknowledgements

This book (just like my last) would not be possible without my friend and editor, Debbie Johnson – the calls, the support, the constant nagging (her words). I appreciate you so incredibly much for being the driving force once again. You are an absolute joy to work with and to have as a friend.

To Donovan and Camille, the honor of being your mother is overwhelming. I'm so proud of the interesting and loving young adults you are becoming. Thank you husband Gregg, for supporting this wild career, busy travel, and sometimes difficult re-entry.

I am lucky enough to call Camille and Jim Holton my parents. They built a foundation of love, trust, hard work, and fun for me to build upon.

Kudos to the Formation Studio crew – Alan Jazak for wrapping his creative brain around these pages.

As always, shout out to my kick-ass crew of friends who make me laugh and inspire me: Tami Evans, Michael Hoffman, Neen James, Lynn Rose, Tina Elve, Leo Cardenas, Tina Barrette, Nikki Nanos, Tim Durkin, Dave Lieber, my National Speakers Association North Texas family, and Lantana golf crew.

I can't forget the amazing audiences and event planners who have allowed me to share my *Good Stuff* on stage for over 20 years. And thanks to you Cool Reader for picking up *It's YOUR Business!*

Your questions, letters, and book-group invitations (I can attend via Skype/Zoom) are always welcome. Drop me a line at Christine@ChristineCashen.com and give me a CEO update.

Yes, that would be you.

—Christine

About the Author

For more than 20 years, Christine Cashen has jazzed an amazing variety of audiences throughout the United States, Canada, South Africa, and Australia. She is an authority on sparking innovative ideas, handling conflict, reducing stress, and energizing employees.

Before hitting the speaking scene, Christine was a university admissions officer, corporate trainer, and broadcaster. She holds a Bachelor's Degree in Communication and a Master's Degree in Adult Education. She is a member of the National Speakers Association and is a Certified Speaking Professional (CSP).

Christine was inducted into the *National Speakers Association, CPAE Speaker Hall of Fame®*, a lifetime achievement award for speaking excellence and professionalism. In 2016, she received an honorary Doctorate Degree from Central Michigan University.

Her book, *THE GOOD STUFF: Quips & Tips on Life, Love, Work and Happiness,* was named motivational book of the year by the Next Generation Indie Book Awards.

Christine resides in Dallas with her husband, their two children, and Murphy, the chocolate lab.

Need a funny and dynamic speaker? Contact Christine@christinecashen.com to find out how she can help make your event an even bigger success!